Family Latin

poems by

Bill Stadick

Finishing Line Press
Georgetown, Kentucky

Family Latin

Copyright © 2020 by Bill Stadick
ISBN 978-1-64662-108-8 First Edition
All rights reserved under International and Pan-American Copyright Conventions. No part of this book may be reproduced in any manner whatsoever without written permission from the publisher, except in the case of brief quotations embodied in critical articles and reviews.

ACKNOWLEDGMENTS

"Sitting on Cuss" and "Rubens Would Need a Light Source" were originally published in *The Christian Century*.
"Greatest Bar Bet of All Time" was originally published in *Conclave*.
"Regarding a Co-Worker's Kindergarten Report Card" was originally published in *First Things*.
"Nunc Dimittis" and "I Thought I Heard the Angels Sing" were originally published in *The Cresset*.
"Syndrome Psalm" was originally published in *Relief Journal*.
"Sleepover at Goya's" was originally published in *The Ekphrastic Review*.

Publisher: Leah Maines
Editor: Christen Kincaid
Cover Art: Scott Stadick and Katie Maule
Author Photo: Tim Evans, Saturn Lounge
Cover Design: Elizabeth Maines McCleavy

Printed in the USA on acid-free paper.
Order online: www.finishinglinepress.com
also available on amazon.com

Author inquiries and mail orders:
Finishing Line Press
P. O. Box 1626
Georgetown, Kentucky 40324
U. S. A.

Table of Contents

The Problem of Veil 1
Sitting on Cuss 2
Probably Not How It Is, But Most Definitely How It
    Sometimes Feels 3
Sleepover at Goya's 4
Girl in Bed in Cab 5
The Day Another Lady Died 6
Imagined Captions for a Muted Politician 7
In the Drive-Thru 8
This Isn't Really about Baseball 9
Greatest Bar Bet of All Time 10
'It's almost as if we sing to one another all day' 11
What Amounts to a Thirty-Second Timeout 12
Between Eight and Nine 13
Another Poem about a Salt Floe Thrown Up by Surging Water .. 14
Poem Writ Whilst Baptists Peaceably Debate
    the Purchase of a $13,897.92 Sound System 15
The Gospel According to Police Procedural 16
Dying Jack's Soliloquy 17
Rubens Would Need a Light Source 18
Nunc Dimittis 20
I Thought I Heard the Angels Sing 21
A Slapdash Translation of Ecclesiastes 22
Syndrome Psalm 23
Regarding a Co-Worker's Kindergarten Report Card 24
Until Then 25
For Selah Someday 26
Family Latin 27

For Judy, Debbie, Rob, Katie and Scott

The Problem of Veil

Let's maybe solve   the problem of *evil*
by treating it as an   anagram because
how hard could it   be really to solve
the problem of   *veil* wouldn't we just
tear it or better   yet have some Upper-
Case One part it   for us and voila every-
thing & I mean every   *vile* thing down to the
last Adolf would make   sense why can't we live
in a world like that   where wordplay solves all

Sitting on Cuss

You come to expect it on the grimy seat,
magic-markered across splitting vinyl
where yellow foam emerges like a new species,
or etched into window glass with the gold teeth
of car keys. In fact, as the bus stumbles you,
transfer in hand, to the back bench, you
almost anticipate the inevitable sitting on cuss
or high school lovehearts or a for-a-good-time-
call-somebody and you no longer pray
for somebody because you know she
may already be somewhere beyond God.
But what you never foresee until it reveals itself
above the green light above the back door
is that HELLO MY NAME IS sticker randomly
pasted by somebody else on his way out,
and you marvel, flat-out, at the dense curlicues
of gang symbol thick-inked into the whitespace
where names like Chip and Laura typically appear.
After city blocks of this, you pull the cord threaded
like a common halo around, above everybody
to let the driver know you have seen enough.

Probably Not How It Is, But Most Definitely How It Sometimes Feels

In my origin narrative there is a deity
                      (sorry, atheists)

but a deafening bang also
                      (apologies, theists)

it being the cacophony of two chunks of
                      (massive, die-shaped)

matter colliding within
                      (crash, boom)

this god's cupped right hand
                      (c'mon, lucky seven)

before being tossed onto the lovely
                      (as lush)

green meadow of a craps table
                      (thud and more thud)

some worlds coming up winner
                      (-winner-chicken-dinner)

I mean megabucks winner
                      (papa, new pair of shoes, done)

but ours snake eyes
                      (beady as Beelzebub)

which is where we find ourselves
                      (parched for an eschatology to cover our losses)

Sleepover at Goya's

    Madrid, 1999

You knew the world wasn't all
Thomas Kinkades when you accepted
his ineluctable invitation,

but lying here in the Prado,
snug-zippered into your bag and staring

at Saturn snarfing a son like a pizza roll,
it's all you can do to game-face it,
make the best of a bad by numbering

each witch on his wall of witches—
one-witch, two-witch—
like counting sheep, you hope
it brings on sleep—
three-witch, no dice.

Hang it,
                it's off to El Greco's to let

The Holy Trinity keep patient watch over
what's left of this dark night of your soul.

Girl in Bed in Cab

They can't see us, but we're right here
with them, picturing the picture—
Lucian Freud's *Girl in Bed*—
taking in NYC from the arms of her
blueblood ex on 12 September 1977

& what wide-eyes sees we see:
a hot mess of the same Big
Apple Mick would soon get all
sprechgesang about (*sha-doo-be*)
from, so the story goes, another cab,

but wide-eyes never blinks,
nor removes resting palm
from temple, not when cabbie calls
for ambulance, not when the first Mrs.
Robert Lowell comes down to check

on the commotion, not even now,
years later, after-hours, as she rests
on a wall at the National Portrait Gallery,
blasé-gazing at a custodian's
absentminded dust-mopping.

The Day Another Lady Died

The day America was sniggering
through another *Andy Griffith Show*,
specifically, the premiere broadcast
of that episode titled, *Rafe Hollister Sings*,
in which a bumpkin moonshiner
turns out to have a dulcet baritone
worthy of representing Mayberry
at a musical competition, at which
he sings, *Look Down That Lonesome
Road*, the 1927 song with music
by Nathaniel Shilkret and lyrics by
Gene Austin (one of the first crooners),
which opens with the lines, *look down,
look down that lonesome road before
you travel on, look up, look up and see
your maker, for Gabriel blows his horn,*
was also the day Lady
Lazarus didn't come forth.

Imagined Captions for a Muted Politician

I am Lord Everything
of the Thralldom
of Solipsism,

elected on a vow
to chase all third
persons from
the land.

Me and myself just
passed a draconian
immigration bill
and, once I sign it
into law,

you will no longer
be welcome
in this poem.

In the Drive-Thru

I am certain
        this minimum wage
                Sappho has much

                to oracle but
        her voice arrives at
my steering wheel so

glitch-mangled all
        that survives
                is [crackle]

                would I [hiss]
        some [frizz]
with [static]

This Isn't Really about Baseball

A fastball when one
is sitting on the curve
followed by a slider

away that catches the
corner when looking
for something up in

the zone before a
culminating change
in the dirt that simply

cannot be resisted
is all that remains to
dear-diary today other

than the requisite grumping
to the dugout while a
mass choir of beer-fueled

boos rains so hard
the grounds crew is
forced to tarp the field.

Greatest Bar Bet of All Time

My one job is *had to*.
My one job is white flag.
My one job is *it's not you,
it's me* text punctuated with
requisite, androgynous,
bawling emoji. My one job
is paddles beside the beloved
and calling it.

      Three downs of snarl
and swagger have moved
not the chains. My one job
is oblong offering end-over-
ending through coliseum air
and even though (greatest
bar bet of all time) no fan
in any fan bar can name
ten of me civilization
could use more of me.

> '**It's almost as if we sing to one another all day.**'
>
> —*Robert Pinsky*

This is the verse I'm blanking to make sure
My colleagues in the hall don't know I hear
Them gossiping.

                It has no lofty goal
To outlast time like *Ozymandias*
Or *Paradise*, once *Lost*, then gained again.
I have no *Urn* to ponder, just this urge
To mask my untoward curiosity.

My fingers pound pentameter so fast
It's difficult to eavesdrop while I type.
Did she, for real, just float *that* simile?
Her last date's ass looked just like what?

Thanks then for that.

                So sweet, their *vers libre*,
Each *entendre*, those makeshift metaphors,
Till, woe betide, this lilting dialogue
Begins to Doppler down the corridor.

This is the verse I'm blanking to make sure
Their singing lasts so long as this poem does.

What Amounts to a Thirty-Second Timeout

Tonight, with some Eagles or other down by four with 9:04 remaining, I power off the flat screen for good and for good reason: my life is nothing *but* scoreboards, including, but not limited to, the imagined tally-marking of sin-sin-sin-sin-sin on heaven's massive white board, the close-of-trading market capitalization of my retirement accounts and that countdown clock next my heart, invisible to radiologists, frenetically subtracting itself to zeroes.

Between Eight and Nine

The expeditionist in me adores
topographic globes, how they
permit a thumb to slide over
(because it's there) an Everest
as though it were a bruise.
It's even easier, Most High, for you

to ride your fingers over the earth—
I feel your breezy breath as you
stroke Wisconsin. How do you
pull it off, convince yourself to
run softly over our lawns on days
like these when everyone's playing

I Love Lucifer in your backyards?
Must you count to ten, letting rage
dissipate between eight and nine,
or check your just fury by repeating
over and over, *remember the plan,
remember the plan, remember...?*

Have you ever had to busy yourself
shoving a block of time into a black
hole to distract your gaze from goings-on?
Whatever you're doing, keep at it.
We'll be needing more occasions
to repent in our next several breaths.

Another Poem about a Salt Floe Thrown up by Surging Water

> Mr. Harris said by telephone from Canada that the Dead Sea was full of salt floes that might have been thrown up by surging water to resemble a female outline. "Hence legend is created out of what can now be explained as a simple geological phenomenon," he said.
> New York Times, December 17, 1995

If only Lot had kept some of his wife
As proof or souvenir, some scraping from

Her lips or hips, a mass of baffling salt.
If only Dorothea Lange were there

To get the shot they'd rave about for years:
The beaten, holy man caught in an act

Of tenderness amid great tragedy.
If only, right? But no. A pity, too,

Because without some evidence, we're down
To God's word versus Mr. Harris's.

Poem Writ Whilst Baptists Peaceably Debate the Purchase of a $13,897.92 Sound System

1 Kings 19:11-12

God bless ye
    4.2 power amps
        for mains and monitors

as well ye
    half-rack dual
        channel frequency

agile receivers
    with four (count
        'em) body packs

but it'll still
    be the still
        small vox

that rocks
    us out that
        piney box

The Gospel According to Police Procedural

O rerun marathon:
    grisly at
    the get-go,
    tidied by
    tops of hours,
    only to
    grisly again.

O rerun marathon:
    same autopsies,
    same perps' heads plunged into
    same squads,
    same demons haunting
    same lip-curling cops on
    same vendettas.

O rerun marathon:
    I've watched
    you long and
    helplessly enough
    to need to find
    a Bible and
    take the deal.

Dying Jack's Soliloquy

Half-smash'd, I still can see thee with my one
Extant isosceles and will be damn'd
If this low flame in my spoon'd skull hath not
Last glints enough to spit across my ruin'd jaw
These several flickers that shall dance like hell
Flames on thy linen superhero cape
And backside of thy hooting Franken-friend
As, guilty-giggling, ye hotfoot it to
Thine homes, high holy days or wheresoe'er
The bless'd flee after beating down the cursed.

Rubens Would Need a Light Source

Advent 1995

They knew.
The famous always know they are watched.
They understood their positions
around the manger mattered, that even
in an unlit cranny of creation, someone
somewhere would record with paint or pen
every head tilt and cow grunt.

Mary, for example, knew. She wrinkled
her pink gown just so, joyed up her eyes just so
and squared her biceps around him just so
for the benefit of Rubens. Then she scurried
over straw for Botticelli's sake and lined up
steer, then steed, then herself, remembering
to clasp her hands just in time above the Lord-Is-Come.

Joseph also knew. He shifted with mock
stage-fright from foot to foot,
glancing at the Messiah as though
a plastic-faced doll
because someday this would serve as model
everywhere for Sunday school pageants.

Even the holy infant knew,
as he squinched his eyes tighter
and tighter, gushing a nimbus
with museum-worthy brilliance
from his pores (Rubens would need
a light source and it might as well be him).

Taking advantage of his useless,
newborn neck muscles, the little
Lord Jesus next experimented
with a series of head flops

to be perfected at some later date
on a hill far away.

Nunc Dimittis

But first another check of the sports scores,
Another walk around my favorite mall,
More purchases at all the swanky stores
And one more game of pickup basketball.
No, wait. There's more. I've only but begun.
Please let me watch another B movie
(I'm thinking maybe *Tremors* or *Top Gun*).
I'd love to drive a Vette that isn't me,
Suck down a sinful, triple-chocolate shake,
Then listen to that silly country tune
That teaches breaky hearts just how to ache.
More grandchildren? Tomorrow's dawn? Next June?
The more I mull, the more desires increase.
It's not so easy to depart in peace.

I Thought I Heard the Angels Sing

Today I almost absalomed my head
While biking to the Kwik-Trip north of Main.
Why would so much of nature have us dead?
Why this proclivity to dole out pain?
By grace alone, I ducked in time to hear
My helmet scrape across the under-bark.
I know this doesn't mean I'm in the clear.
I've read my Eliot, *O dark dark dark*.
But I'll take any break that comes my way,
Each non-malignancy and whoa-close call
Between right now and *let's call it a day*.
If the ride must end, I'm predisposed to stall,
To stop my ears when I hear heavenly choirs,
To ask the bug-eyed reaper, *where's the fire?*

A Slapdash Translation of Ecclesiastes

Pause the commemorative DVD on the boy in blue-face,
that one, arms in air, mid-hoot, who's rocking every minute

of our girls' aught-seven state championship. It's easier *now*
to see what Omniscience could see in the moment, that the boy

had, what, a year left, not four-score-and-actuarial-change,
that the line would snake around Hafemeister's and down Market,

that a time to dance and a time to mourn would be separated
by no time at all. We can unpause now, let things play out

as we know they will, then slip the disc back into its sleeve
with our illusions intact that we're somehow running this show.

Syndrome Psalm

(for Selah Noel)

Funny   there is a patron saint of television (Clare)
                     but no patron saint of Maple Syrup
                     Urine Disease sufferers.

Odd   there is a patron saint of brewers (Nicholas)
                     but no patron saint of those wracked
                     by lysosomal storage anomalies.

Random   there is a patron saint of poets (see stanza 4)
                     but no patron saint of the negligible few
                     with 17q21.31 microdeletion syndrome.

Rare   how he alone is on call to help me (Columba)
                     draft prayers on behalf of the x-in-a-million
                     including the x in this tube-tangled incubator.

Regarding a Co-Worker's Kindergarten Report Card

(For Debbie)

The nun, you said,
bad-marked your report card
because you could not
answer *why, why, why*
God made her or you
or them or me.
All jowls and rules,
that woman. As if
the motives of God
were true-false, multiple
choice or kindergarten simple.

—So why did he?

I knew you would ask
and seem to remember penning
the answer somewhere:
the inside of my left wrist,
the toe of my right sneaker
or was it the cardback
of my spiral notebook?
I cannot locate the eternal
plan just now, but I did know.

I really must have.

Just look across my office.
See in the corner of my cluttered, trivial desk
that miracle of smirk playing itself out
on my daughter's kindergarten face.

Until Then

(For Debbie)

*Sinatra told Hugh Martin, "The name of my album is
A Jolly Christmas. Do you think you could jolly up that line
for me?" Martin's new line was "Hang a shining star upon
the highest bough." Martin made several other alterations,
changing the song's focus to a celebration of present happiness,
rather than anticipation of a better future.*
                Have Yourself a Merry Little Christmas Wikipedia
                Entry 12/25/17

I can't, not this Christmas, jolly up any lines.
There are department store loudspeakers for that.

Neither can I make merry with jingling words,
not when another celebration of the Word

become flesh must now also commemorate
a once-gestating body become group text.

I cannot jolly up these lines,
nor hang star upon highest bough,

but I can bow
in hope against shining hope

that *someday soon, we all will be together,*
according to the Gospel of promise,

and I can embolden any of us
with ears to hear that

*until then we'll have to
muddle through somehow.*

For Selah Someday

It's me: your welcome-to-the-planet poem.
I know I will be lost then found then lost
Then found then left you-can't-remember-where.
I understand I might be nothing more
Than *something grampy wrote when I was born.*
I know how many decades it might take
For you to dig into that drawer and start
To read about the eyepatches and tubes,
That NIC-U night you lost your breath, the O
MGs of thanks you found it just in time.
It's me: your welcome-to-the-timeline poem.
I know how far from right now someday is
And I've got nothing else to do but wait.

Family Latin

Likely not, but if any joint filers and their several dependents
are still wanting a little Latin to work onto their tankards
or needle into their pillows, they could do worse than cop
coelum qui tueri from the Balls of Fredericksburg, i.e.
heaven for those who dare.

                        It's the ultimate throwback
throwdown to be spelled out on the fridge in primary-color
letter magnets, a self-taunt to goad the tribe into numbering
their days as though the fool things might prove numberless.

Bill Stadick has published poetry, fiction and creative nonfiction in various publications, including *The Windhover, First Things, Conclave, The Christian Century, The Ekphrastic Review, Christianity and Literature, Barren Magazine* and *The Cresset*. His work also appears in the poetry anthologies, *Imago Dei: Poems from Christianity and Literature* (Abingdon Press, 2012), and *In a Strange Land* (Wipf and Stock, 2019). He founded and writes for Page 17, a marketing communications firm.

www.ingramcontent.com/pod-product-compliance
Lightning Source LLC
LaVergne TN
LVHW041511070426
835507LV00012B/1495